Pirates

Mick Gowar

OXFORD
UNIVERSITY PRESS

OXFORD
UNIVERSITY PRESS

Great Clarendon Street, Oxford OX2 6DP

Oxford University Press is a department of the University of Oxford.
It furthers the University's objective of excellence in research, scholarship,
and education by publishing worldwide in

Oxford   New York

Auckland   Cape Town   Dar es Salaam   Hong Kong   Karachi
Kuala Lumpur   Madrid   Melbourne   Mexico City   Nairobi
New Delhi   Shanghai   Taipei   Toronto

With offices in

Argentina   Austria   Brazil   Chile   Czech Republic   France   Greece
Guatemala   Hungary   Italy   Japan   Poland   Portugal   Singapore
South Korea   Switzerland   Thailand   Turkey   Ukraine   Vietnam

Oxford is a registered trade mark of Oxford University Press
in the UK and in certain other countries

British Library Cataloguing in Publication Data

Data available

ISBN 978-0-19-917939-8

7 9 10 8 6

Printed in China by Imago

Paper used in the production of this book is a natural,
recyclable product made from wood grown in sustainable forests.
The manufacturing process conforms to the environmental
regulations of the country of origin.

Acknowledgements

The publisher would like to thank the following for permission to reproduce
photographs: **p10** Getty/AFP, **p11** Corbis/Jeffrey L Rotman, **p12** Corbis, **p13** The National Archives,
p15 Ancient Art & Architecture, **p17** Mary Evans Picture Library, **p19** Corbis/Bettmann, **p22**cr
Alamy/Popperfoto, **p23**tr Mary Evans Picture Library, **p24** Corbis/Bettmann, **p28** Kobal/Walt Disney
Pictures, **p29**t Donald Cooper/Photostage, **p30** Alamy/Iain Masterton

Cover artwork by Brian Lee

Illustrations by: **p4**, **p5**, **p6**, **p7**, **p8**, **p9**, **p10**, **p14**, **p16**, **p18**, **p20**, **p22**, **p23**, **p25**, **p27**, **p29** Brian Lee

Design by John Walker

Every effort has been made to contact copyright holders of material reproduced in this book. If notified,
the publishers will be pleased to rectify any errors or omissions at the earliest opportunity

Contents

Introduction

Since people first started sailing across the seas there have been pirates trying to rob them. Two thousand years ago, there were pirates in the Mediterranean attacking Greek and Roman ships. These Pirates made a lot of money from ransoming wealthy passengers as well as from the cargoes.

When Julius Caesar was a young man he borrowed lots of money that he couldn't pay back. Caesar got on a ship to Greece to get away from his creditors and because he was also hoping to borrow more money from some rich Greeks. A few days later his boat was attacked by pirates.

Instead of being frightened, Caesar treated the whole thing as a huge joke.

Roman galley under sail.

"When the pirates demanded a ransom of twenty talents Caesar burst out laughing. They did not know, he said, who it was they had captured, and he volunteered to pay them fifty. For thirty eight days he joined in all their games and exercises as if he were their leader, instead of their prisoner. He also wrote poems and speeches which he read aloud to them, and if they failed to admire his work he would call them **illiterate** savages to their faces and would often laughingly threaten to have them all hanged."

Plutarch, *Parallel Lives*

As soon as his ransom was paid and he was released, Caesar borrowed even more money, chartered a fleet of ships and sailed off to catch the pirates. He found them sailing off the coast of Greece, took them prisoner and dragged them ashore to be tried by the local **magistrates**. When the magistrates hesitated, Caesar took the prisoners back and crucified them all.

Caesar takes the law into his own hands.

Viking pirates

Originally, the word 'Viking' was not the name of a people or group of peoples: it was an old Norse word meaning a pirate raid. Going 'a-Viking' meant to sail away to steal and kill.

The Vikings' favourite targets were monasteries, because there was lots to steal: for example, the jewels, gold and silver on the covers of bibles and holy books; the silver or gold crucifixes in monastery churches; the gold and silver cups and plates used in services.

One of the first Viking raids against Britain was in AD 793 when vikings attacked the island of Lindisfarne off the Northumbrian coast.

Rich pickings could be plundered from a monastery.

Witness box

"They came to the church of Lindisfarne, laid everything waste with grievous plundering, trampled the holy places with polluted feet, dug up the altars and seized all the treasures of the holy church. They killed some of the brothers; some they took away with them in fetters; many they drove out, naked and loaded with insults; and some they drowned in the sea."

Simon of Durham

The Vikings were fierce fighters, but they could be
beaten. In AD 1171, the Viking chief Svein Asleifson and
his men captured Dublin. The people of the town
begged for time to gather together enough treasure to
pay Svein to go away and leave them alone. He agreed
to give them one night. In the morning, when the
Vikings came to meet the town's leaders, they saw a
great treasure spread out on the ground in front of them.
What they didn't see, in their haste to get the treasure,
were the deep concealed pits that the Dubliners had dug
during the night. The Vikings fell into the pits and were
killed.

Falling into the trap.

Spanish gold

Three hundred to four hundred years ago, Britain, France, Portugal, Holland and Spain all had huge **empires**, and the treasure from their colonies was brought back to Europe by ship.

Three hundred years ago there was no radio for ships to call for help if they were attacked and no helicopters to come to their rescue. A treasure ship could be all alone, in the middle of the ocean — a sitting target!

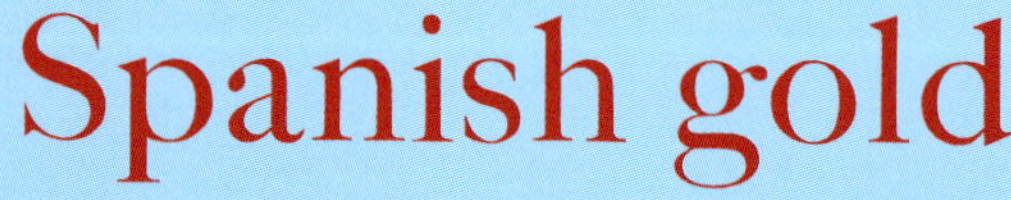

Since 1492, when Columbus first sailed to the islands of Cuba and Haiti in the Caribbean and claimed them for the King and Queen of Spain, Spanish soldiers had conquered most of Central and South America and much of what is now the United States. The Spanish invaders were amazed at the gold and silver jewellery the people wore and the wonderful golden statues and masks in their temples. This is part of a list of some of the treasure Hernan Cortes, the conqueror of Mexico, stole and sent back to the King of Spain:

Witness box

"First a large gold wheel with a design of monsters on it... this weighing as much as 3,800 ounces of gold... Two necklaces of gold and stone mosaic, one of which has eight strings of 232 red jewels and 163 green jewels... the other necklace has four strings of 102 red jewels and 172 which appear to be green in colour... Two birds with green plumage and their feet, beaks and eyes made of gold... A large alligator head in gold... A helmet of blue stone mosaic with twenty small gold bells hanging round the outside."

Cortes, *Letters from Mexico*

Conquistadors stealing gold.

Making coins

Turning treasure into coins.

The Spaniards in the Caribbean began turning the gold and silver they found into coins and sending it back to Spain. The coins they minted became famous as pirate loot: pieces-of-eight and doubloons.

Pieces-of-eight, or pesos, were made from an ounce of silver. They were worth eight reales (Spanish silver pennies), which is how they got the nickname 'pieces-of-eight'. On one side of the coin was the Spanish coat of arms; on the other was a strange sign of two circles which stood for the two worlds, Old and New (Europe and America). On either side of those two circles were two lines representing the Pillars of Hercules (the old-fashioned name for the Straits of Gibraltar) which were thought to be the gateway between the Old World of Europe and the New World of America.

Pieces-of-eight

This symbol became so well known that when the United States of America was formed, the new government took the old sign of the circles and pillars on the back of the pieces-of-eight and used it as the basis of the sign for their new currency, the dollar.

The most valuable Spanish coin was the doubloon, which was made from an ounce of solid gold (which would be worth about £450 now). The correct name for the doubloon was the two-escudo piece, which was how it got its name: it was worth *double one* escudo = doubloon.

Doubloons and gold bars found in the wreck of a 17th century Spanish ship.

When is a pirate not a pirate?

Answer: When he's a Drake.

One of the greatest thieves of Spanish gold was Sir Francis Drake.

Drake is well known for helping to defeat the Spanish Armada in 1588, but his most daring exploit was between 1577 and 1580 when he sailed round the world stealing treasure from Spanish ships.

A replica of Drake's ship, The Golden Hind.

On his way round the world Drake attacked Spanish towns and ships, and when he returned to England he gave Queen Elizabeth I the treasure he'd captured. Drake's treasure today would be worth more than £85 million pounds. The Queen let Drake keep treasure worth nearly £2 million for himself and £1.5 million for his crew.

Spain and England were at war for much of the time that Drake was attacking Spanish treasure ships, and Drake was a privateer, a sort of legal pirate who was given permission to attack enemy ships in times of war. Privateers were given letters of marque, originally signed by the king or queen, that said that the bearer of the letter was an official privateer and not a pirate. Each letter also stated which nations' ships they were permitted to attack. That meant that if a privateer was caught by the enemy, they should be treated as a prisoner of war and not as a pirate – pirates were normally hanged as soon as they were caught. A *letter of marque* could mean the difference between life and death if a privateer was captured by the enemy's navy, or even by their own navy.

Permission to attack!

Other types of pirates

Corsairs

'Corsair' was the name given to pirates who robbed shipping in the Mediterranean. They mainly sailed from the North African ports of Algeria and Tunis and were given permission by the rulers of the Muslim countries of North Africa to attack Christian shipping. But there were also Christian corsairs, sent out by the knights of St John of Malta to attack the ships of Muslim countries.

Barbary corsair

Buccaneers

The original buccaneers weren't pirates at all; they were French hunters who lived on the islands of Hispaniola and Tortuga (now part of Haiti) in the Caribbean. They made a poor living from hunting the wild cattle that lived on these islands. They became known as buccaneers because they cured their meat by cooking and drying it over a sort of barbecue, a trick they'd learned from the Arawak Indians who lived on the islands. The old French word for this type of cooking was 'boucan', so these hunters became known as 'boucaniers', or, as English people pronounced it, 'buccaneers'.

When Spanish soldiers tried to drive them off the islands in the 1600s, the buccaneers joined up with French and British pirates and privateers to attack Spanish treasure ships. So they had their revenge, and piracy was a much better way of earning a good living than hunting wild cattle and eating dried meat.

Maybe because the word buccaneer sounds tough, strong and thrilling, it became the name of any Caribbean pirate. The word 'buccaneer' is sometimes used today to describe someone like a businessman who is particularly ruthless or daring.

A pirate's life for me?

Being a pirate wasn't an easy life. Working on any sort of ship in the 1600s and 1700s was very tough. There were lots of hard, dangerous jobs that had to be done. Sailors, and pirates too, had to climb up slippery masts and wet rigging in storms and gales to take down the sails.

If anyone fell and broke an arm or leg, there was only one remedy: cut it off before it went bad. That's why the popular picture of a pirate is a man with only one leg – like Long John Silver in *Treasure Island*.

Not all plain sailing.

Pirates of fiction echoed the reality of a dangerous lifestyle.

However, being a pirate was usually better than serving in the
navy or on a **merchant ship**. Sailors on both **navy ships** and
merchant ships were often cruelly flogged for small wrongs, and
food and pay were very poor.

A life at sea could be very hard.

Many pirates were **mutineers**
who had taken over the ship
of a cruel or unjust captain.
Pirates often treated the
captains of ships they
captured particularly badly if
they found out they'd been
mistreating their men.

Witness box

"Their reasons for going a-pirating being to revenge
themselves on base merchants and cruel
commanders, they would often enquire into the
commander's treatment of his men... one of the
favourite torments inflicted on captured captains
was 'the sweats'. He was made to run round and
round the mizzenmast between decks to the tune of
a merry jig while he was encouraged to go faster by
the surrounding pirates jabbing his backside with
points of Swords, Penknives, Compasses, Forks..."
Cordingley, *Life Among The Pirates*

A pirate crew

Every pirate ship had a captain who was elected by the rest of the crew. The captain was often the fiercest fighter; someone the rest of the crew feared and respected. They had total command of the ship when it was in battle and could punish pirates who disobeyed orders or broke the rules of the ship.

The quartermaster was second in command and was in charge of all the food and water supplies. He had to organise rationing when supplies ran low. The quartermaster usually led the attacks on other ships.

Pirates attacked without mercy.

Next in importance was the sailing master, or navigator. Many sailing masters were officers from navy or merchant ships who were forced into piracy when their ships were captured.

In 1822, Aaron Smith was on a ship captured by pirates. He was first mate and an experienced navigator, but the pirates forced him to become their ship's surgeon as well. At first he refused. This is how the pirate captain persuaded Aaron to join his crew:

Pirates showed their prisoners no mercy.

Pirate attack

Although they are often portrayed in films and books as swashbuckling and romantic, pirates were vicious and violent criminals. Many pirates did not hesitate to kill anyone who could be a witness against them.

The dangers of travelling by sea.

In 1825, Lucretia Parker was a passenger on the
Eliza-Ann, a small ship sailing to Antigua in the
West Indies. The ship was attacked by Cuban
pirates, and this is part of a letter Lucretia wrote to
her brother describing what happened. In this part
of the letter, Lucretia is telling her brother what the
pirates did to the crew of the Eliza-Ann:

"Having first divested them of every article of
clothing but their shirts and trousers, with swords,
knives, axes, etc., they fell on the unfortunate crew
of the Eliza-Ann with the ferocity of cannibals! In
vain did they beg for mercy and entreat their
murderers to spare their lives! In vain did poor
Captain Smith attempt to touch their feelings and
to move them to pity by [telling them] he had a
wife and three small children at home wholly
dependent on him for support. But alas, the poor
man entreated in vain... Having received a heavy
blow from one with an axe, he snapped the cords
with which he was bound and attempted to escape
by flight, but was met by another of the ruffians,
who plunged a knife or dirk into his heart! I stood
near him at this moment and was covered with his
blood — on receiving the fatal wound he gave a
single groan and fell lifeless at my feet."

Letter from Lucretia Parker to her brother,
reprinted **Cordingly**, *Life Among The Pirates*

Scourges of the seven seas

WANTED

Svein Asleifson

Also called *The Ultimate Viking*, Svein was a Viking chieftain who lived on the Isle of Orkney and combined farming with leading pirate raids on the coasts of Scotland and Ireland.

Witness box

"He would go off plundering in the Hebrides and in Ireland on what he called his 'spring-trip', then back home just after mid-summer, where he stayed till the cornfields had been reaped and the grain was safely in. After that he would go off raiding again and never came back till the first month of winter was ended. This he used to call his 'autumn-trip'".

Orkneyinga Saga

WANTED

Aruj and Khayr ad-Din

These pirates were nicknamed the Barbarossa Brothers because of their red beards, from the Italian words 'barba' (beard) and 'rossa' (red). They were two Muslim Greek brothers who became corsairs, sailing mainly from the port of Algiers. Khayr ad-Din was such a successful pirate that he was made commander of the Turkish navy (a sort of Mediterranean Francis Drake).

WANTED

Henry Morgan

The best known leader of the buccaneers wasn't a Frenchman, but a Welshman: Captain Henry Morgan. Morgan didn't just attack Spanish ships, he attacked towns and forts too, including the city of Panama. Morgan always claimed he wasn't a pirate but a privateer, and when a book was published saying he was a pirate, Morgan sued for libel and won. Morgan became not only famous but also very rich and was knighted by King Charles II.

WANTED

Francois l'Ollonois

He was one of the original buccaneers. When all the other hunters in his group were killed by Spanish soldiers, l'Ollonois became a pirate to have his revenge. In one incident he forced one captured Spanish sailor to eat the heart of another. In the end he was given a taste of his own medicine: he was captured by cannibals in Panama who cooked and ate him!

Edward Teach (aka Blackbeard)

Blackbeard was one of the most ferocious looking pirates. Just before an attack, he plaited slow-burning fuses into his hair and beard. When his ship was eventually captured, Blackbeard was shot five times, had twenty serious sword wounds, but didn't collapse until a highland soldier cut off his head! Some sailors said that when Blackbeard's headless body was thrown into the water, it swam round the ship three times before sinking. The naval commander tied Blackbeard's head onto the front of his ship like a carved figurehead. Then he sailed back to Virginia to claim the reward for killing Blackbeard.

Mrs Cheng

One of the most successful pirates of all time was a woman: Mrs Cheng. She was married to a Chinese pirate chief and when he died in 1807, Mrs Cheng took over command of his fleet. She married her husband's second in command, Chang Pao, and together they ran a pirate navy of over three hundred ships and thousands of pirates. They terrorised the towns and villages along the coast of South China and up the Pearl River.

When Mrs Cheng and Chang Pao finally surrendered, their pirate fleet was so large and powerful that the Chinese government didn't dare to punish them. Chang Pao became an officer in the Chinese army and Mrs Cheng opened a **casino**.

The greatest pirate books, plays and films

Since the 1700s stories about pirates have been very popular. Now there are pirate films as well. Sometimes the pirates are the villains and sometimes they are the heroes and heroines. Here's a selection of famous fictional pirates for you to enjoy.

Treasure Island is the story of a search for hidden pirate treasure which starts when a map is discovered in the sea chest of a dead pirate.

The book itself started with a map, too.

Robert Louis Stevenson was on holiday in Scotland with his wife, his parents and his young stepson, Lloyd Osbourne. The weather was terrible, but at least Lloyd had a new paintbox to amuse him. One rainy afternoon, Stevenson came and sat at the table where Lloyd was painting, took a brush and began to paint a map of an imaginary island.

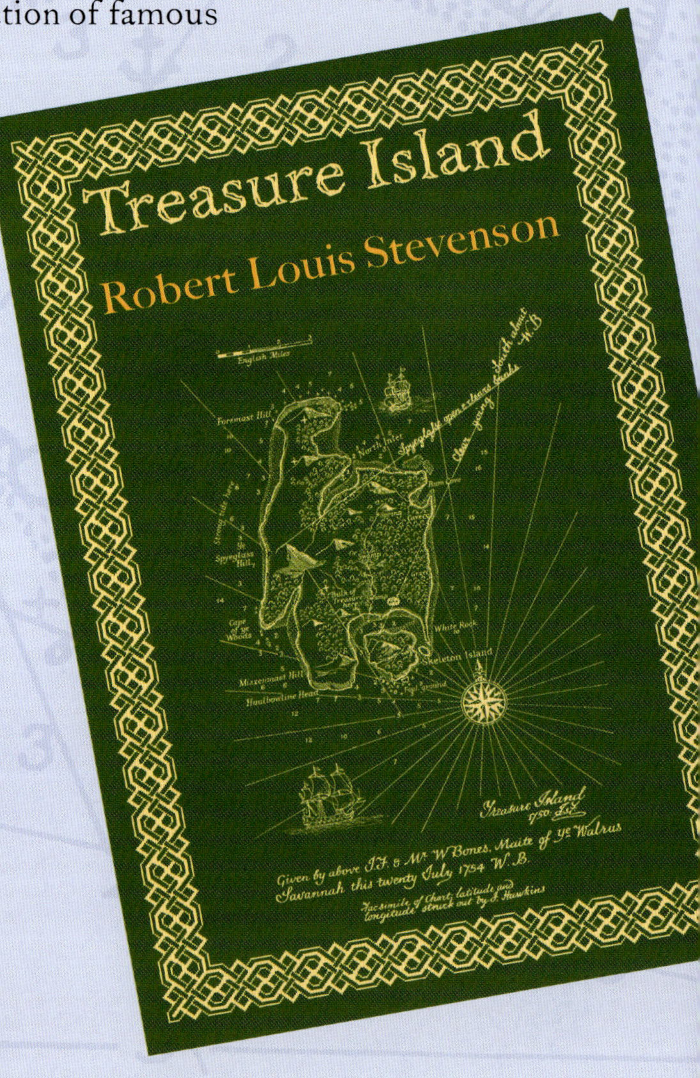

Many years later Lloyd Osbourne wrote:

"I shall never forget the thrill of Skeleton Hill, Spyglass Hill, nor the heart-stirring climax of the three red crosses! And the greater climax still when he wrote down the words 'Treasure Island' at the top right-hand corner! And he seemed to know so much about it too — the pirates, the buried treasure, the man who had been **marooned** on the island."

Introduction and notes to **Oxford University Press Edition**, *Treasure Island*, 1900.

The most memorable character in the book is the bloodthirsty Long John Silver, the one-legged cook, who turns out to be the ex-quartermaster of Captain Flint, the pirate whose treasure lies buried on Treasure Island.

Pirates of the Caribbean: The Curse of The Black Pearl, Walt Disney Films

Jack Sparrow used to be captain of The Black Pearl, a pirate ship, until the villainous Barbossa, Jack's second in command, stole Jack's ship, all his treasure and left him marooned on a desert island. Jack wants his treasure back, but what he doesn't know is that the gold Barbossa stole from him is Aztec gold, and there is a terrible curse on anyone who owns it. Can Jack get his gold back without falling victim to the curse?

Peter Pan

by J M Barrie

Captain Hook, the villain of J M Barrie's play Peter Pan, isn't looking for treasure like Long John Silver. Hook is obsessed with taking revenge on Peter Pan and avoiding an enormous crocodile which is trying to eat him. In a past fight, Peter Pan cut Hook's right hand off and fed it to the crocodile. The crocodile liked the taste so much that he's been pursuing Hook ever since, in the hope of eating the rest of him.

Piratica

By Tanith Lee

Art Blastside is a young girl who has lost her memory and has been put into a dreadful boarding school by her father. As her memory slowly comes back she remembers that her mother was a pirate. Art runs away from school to find her mother's old crew, but finds them on board a fake pirate ship making advertisements for Pirate Coffee. Was Art's mother just an actress who once played the part of a pirate, or was she the heroine that Art believes she was?

Modern piracy

A modern day pirate.

Although the word 'pirate' or 'piracy' usually means robbery at sea, there are many different sorts of pirates and piracy. Nowadays piracy also means copying or **counterfeiting** something someone else has made.

Are you a pirate or a victim?

Have you ever:

1. copied a CD on your computer and given it or sold it to a friend?

2. bought a bottle of perfume or watch with a designer name from a street trader and found it wasn't the genuine article?

3. copied an article from an encyclopedia or the Internet and handed it in for homework without changing it?

4. copied a picture or illustration from a website without paying to use it?

5. bought a video which had really bad picture and sound quality?

6. sung *Happy Birthday To You* at a birthday party which wasn't in someone's home?

Turn the book upside down to read the answers.

If you answered 'yes' to questions 1, 3, 4 or 6 you are a pirate. All those things are protected by copyright, which means you can't copy or perform them without paying a fee to the people who originally wrote the song or article, or made the picture or photograph. If you answered 'yes' to 2 or 5, you're lucky – modern pirates don't make their victims walk the plank, but you are still a victim of piracy!

Glossary

aka – stands for 'also known as' – if someone has a nickname or another name they use to hide their true identity

casino – a place, often part of a hotel, where gambling games like roulette and poker are played

conquistadors – the Spanish soldiers who conquered much of Central and South America in the 16th and 17th centuries

counterfeit – a fake which is a copy of something valuable: for example, copies of money, jewellery, or designer labelled goods like perfume or watches

empire – a group of countries or nations ruled by one monarch or president. For example, the Roman Empire covered most of Europe, North Africa and the Middle East. The British Empire included Australia, India, Canada, New Zealand and many African nations

illiterate – someone who can't read or write

magistrate – someone who is not a trained lawyer or judge who tries minor cases and disputes. Magistrates act as both judge and jury, deciding whether an accused person is guilty or not guilty and, if they are guilty, what their punishment should be

marooned – the punishment for a pirate who stole from his crewmates or ran away during a fight. The pirate was left alone on an island, with just a bottle of water and a loaded pistol, but with no way to escape

merchant ship – a ship carrying cargo owned by a company or a merchant

monastery – a place where a community of monks live together according to strict rules. Each day is divided into periods of prayer, rest and work

mutineer – a soldier, sailor or airman who rebels against his commanding officers. Mutineers on a ship often set the captain and anyone loyal to him adrift in an open boat

naval ship – a ship owned by a monarch or government, or a warship

Index